On Writing Words

BOOKS BY KALINDA ROSE STEVENSON

Book Writing Made Simple Series

Book Writing Made Simple (Volume 1): How to Start Writing a
Book with the Right Question

Book Writing Made Simple (Volume 2): How One Question
Can Eliminate Your Greatest Obstacle to Writing Your
Book

Book Writing Made Simple (Volume 3): Do You Know What
Your Reader Really Wants?

Other Writing Books

Book Writing Made Simple 3-in-1: How to Write a Book the
Simple Way

On Writing Words: A Writer's Essential Relations with Words.

Writer's Block and Your True Self: 4 Questions to Banish
Writer's Block

Does the Bible Really Say That? Series

Your True Self Identity: How Familiar Translations of Bible
Verses in the Gospel of Matthew Hide Your True Identity
from You

Gospel of Wealth or Poverty? How Do Bible Verses about
Jesus, Wealth, Poverty, and Heaven Affect Your Income?

Kindle Mini Books

Does Positive Thinking Work? When Positive Affirmations
Aren't Enough to Change Your Life

The Hidden Reason Why You Are Stuck: A True Story about
the Difference between Success and Failure

On Writing Words

A Writer's Essential Relations With Words

Kalinda Rose Stevenson, Ph.D.

Author of

Book Writing Made Simple Series

Published by ABKA Publishing, North Las Vegas, Nevada

ISBN-13: 978-0615987682

ISBN-10: 0615987680

Cover design by Kalinda Rose Stevenson and James L. Stevenson

Cover Image: Chambered Nautilus, 123RF Stock Photos

This publication is designed to provide accurate and authoritative information in regard to the subject matter covered. It is sold with the understanding that the publisher is not engaged in rendering legal, accounting, or other professional services. If legal advice or other expert assistance is required, the services of a competent professional person should be sought.

Library of Congress Control Number: 2014904799

This book is dedicated with gratitude to the memories of my elementary school teachers who taught me to read and write.

A writer is a person who enters into sustained relations with the language for experiment and experience not available in any other way.

William Stafford

Contents

Preface: Learning to Write xi

Introduction: Making Language Visible 1

Chapter 1: Relations with Words 7

Chapter 2: Relations or Relationship? 11

Chapter 3: Word by Word.................................... 25

Chapter 4: Using Words 29

Chapter 5: Words as Teachers 35

Chapter 6: Words Separate.................................. 45

Chapter 7: The Right Words................................. 53

Chapter 8: Making Words Invisible........................ 61

Chapter 9: Private Words and Public Words........ 65

Conclusion 69

References... 73

About the Author... 75

Index 77

Preface
Learning to Write

When I think of the greatest gifts of my life, learning to read and write have to be close to the top of the list.

I grew up in almost bookless family. Actually, there were a few pornographic books my brothers and I weren't supposed to know about tucked away in the rafters in the cellar. We didn't have children's books. I have a vague memory of my mother reading stories a few times from the rarely used Childcraft books on a shelf, but listening to bedtime stories was never a regular part of our lives. I never remember seeing my mother read a book. My father read his porn behind the closed bathroom door.

The tiny town where I grew up had a public library—two small adjoining rooms with a meager selection of books that was open between one and four on Saturday afternoons and between seven and nine on Tuesday evenings. I didn't know about it until I was in elementary school.

There was no public kindergarten in the town. This was long before the era of Sesame Street when puppets teach the alphabet to very young children. I had already reached the ripe old age of six before I learned the letters of the alphabet.

I used to watch my mother sit at the kitchen table and write letters. I wondered about the strange shapes on paper. I wanted to know what those strange shapes meant. I wanted to know what she knew. I wanted to know how to make those strange shapes myself.

Then I started first grade the day after my sixth birthday. My teacher never smiled and seemed to despise children. Yet, my unsmiling, harsh teacher gave me one of the greatest gifts of my life. She taught me how to crack the code. She taught me how to read and she taught me how to write. I could look at strange shapes on paper and know them by name. I was excited to learn to read and I was even more excited to learn to write.

I remember sitting at my desk in school with

sheets of double-lined paper in front of me, as we learned how to print the letters of the alphabet. I loved it. I loved knowing how to make those big shapes on the double-lined paper. I loved knowing the names of those shapes.

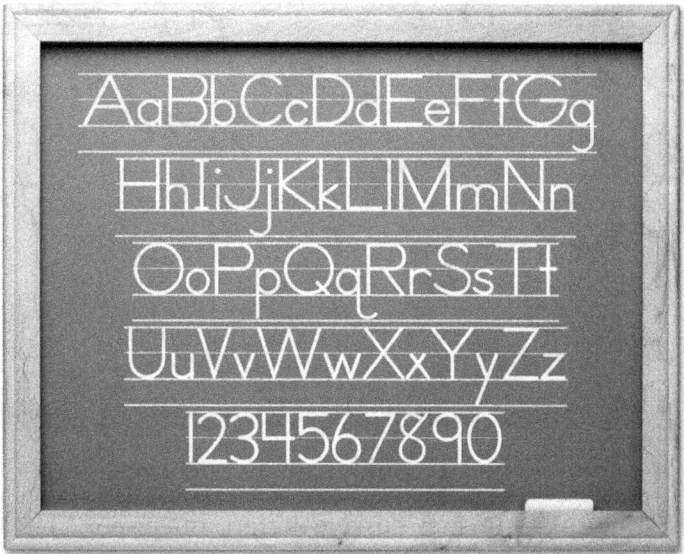

It was wondrous. I could write.

I don't remember whether I was in the second or third grade when another grim-faced, unsmiling teacher taught me to write with the Rinehart Method of cursive writing. (Until the fifth grade, all of my elementary school teachers were stern, strict, unsmiling women.) In class, we spent a lot of time practicing our letters, to produce exactly the right curves and swoops and flourishes on our double-lined paper.

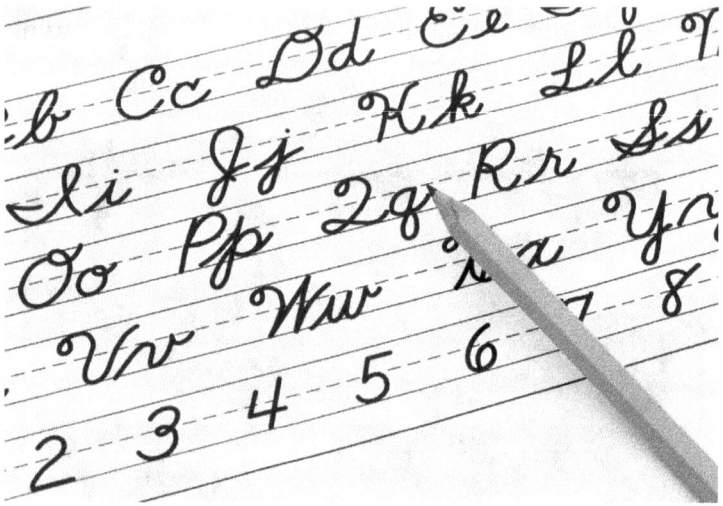

My mother's cursive handwriting was no longer a mystery to me. I could read it and even better, I could write my own cursive letters on paper. Then, and only then, I knew I had deciphered the mystery. I knew how to read and write.

A Practical Purpose

On Writing Words: A Writer's Essential Relations with Words is not about techniques of writing, but about your relationship to written language. If this sounds too academic, be assured that my purpose is profoundly practical. Your skill as a writer depends upon the words you use. The better you know your words, the better your writing will become.

And before you assume that I am encouraging you to expand your vocabulary with more and more words, that is not at all what I mean.

What I do mean is that you get to know the words you use all the time without thinking about them and to think of the words you use as your teachers as well as your tools.

As you get to know your words better, you can expand your appreciation of what it means to you that you can not only read, you can also write. As a writer, you can use your writing skills for more than jotting down a list of items to buy at the supermarket. You can write words that can deeply influence the lives of other people, people you will never meet, people who live in places you will never see. You can write words that will endure long after you. You can use your words to make life better for other people.

My underlying premise is that the more you know about the words you use, the better you will be able to use them to write clearly and effectively to enhance the lives of your readers and to fulfill your own dreams for becoming a writer.

Introduction
Making Language Visible

Write (*verb*)
To form letters or numbers on a surface with a pen, pencil, etc.
To create (a book, poem, story, etc.) by writing words on paper, on a computer, etc.
To produce (a written document, agreement, rule, etc.) by writing (Merriam-Webster).

Who Is a Writer?

What do you have to do to claim the identity of *writer?* In common usage, the designation of writer applies to people whose work is to write creations such as books, articles, poems, and stories. A broader definition is that a writer is anyone who writes. The first definition is defined by the result of writing; the second by the process of writing itself.

On Writing Words: A Writer's Essential Relations with Words is intended for people who write or aspire to write creations such as books, articles, poems, and stories. However, the focus is on the essential relationship between a writer and

1

written language.

The Essential Relationship

Before we consider the relationship between a writer and written language, let's focus on the word that's easiest to overlook in the title, the adjective *essential*. In contemporary English, essential means "extremely important and necessary" (Merriam-Webster).

This definition of the adjective doesn't quite capture the meaning of the noun form *essence*. Consider how Merriam-Webster defines essence:

> Essence (noun)
> The basic nature of a thing
> The quality or qualities that make a thing what it is.

The Latin root is *essentia* ("being or essence of something"). Essence is what makes something what it is. This means that *essential* has a deeper meaning than "important and necessary." Essential refers to the basic nature of something.

In this case, the focus is on the defining essence of a writer. What makes a writer a writer? If you are a writer, you are defined by a particular relationship with language. You are writer because you put words into some medium, whether the medium is paper or a computer or something else. This is your defining essence.

Your relationship with language is *essential*—not because it is extremely important and necessary, but because the essential nature of being a writer is that you write. You can be a writer even if what you write is neither extremely important nor necessary. However, you cannot be a writer unless you are in a particular relationship with language. This relationship is the essence of what it means to be a writer.

Why Writing Exists

Language is any system of words or signs that that people use to communicate with each other. The English word *language* is derived from the Latin word, *lingua,* which means "tongue." All human language began with spoken words. Writing came much, much later than spoken language in human history.

When and where and how human beings began to write is a fascinating study but those questions can distract us from asking an even more basic question. *Why* did our ancestors begin to write?

Our human ancestors wanted to save words in a medium that lasted longer than spoken words. When you speak a word, only those close enough to hear you can know what you said. Even if they hear it, they might not remember it. You might not remember what you said either. Speak a word and it is gone. Write it down and it can last forever.

Throughout the world, throughout history, in most cultures of the world, people developed different systems to make their spoken words permanent. The dominant motivation was the same. Writing fulfills a desire to make impermanent spoken words permanent by turning ephemeral spoken words into enduring written words. Writing can also make what is local become universal.

Writing Makes Language Visible

Writing does this because it makes language visible.

The spoken words are represented by pictures or symbols or letters drawn or scratched or written or printed on some sort of medium. The medium can be a long-lasting substance, such as a clay tablet baked in the sun. It can be as short-lived as sand on a beach with a rising tide. It can be as fragile as parchment or as durable as granite. Whatever the medium, written language expands the boundaries of language to include both written and spoken words.

In a literate culture, where most of us learn to write as children, the act of writing is one of those skills we take for granted. You learn to walk, you learn to feed yourself, you learn to tie your shoes, you learn to write. Writing is just one of those skills we learn and then don't think about after we have mastered the skill.

Benefits of Writing

Just as you have no reason to stop and consider how valuable it is to you to be able to walk, feed yourself, or tie your shoes—unless injury or illness prevents you from doing these simple actions—you have little reason to stop and think about the extraordinary activity called writing and the great benefits writing brings to all of us as human beings. Writing your books or stories or poems is possible because you can write.

How well you write is not just a matter of your imagination and skill at telling stories or laying out information in a compelling way. How well you write is deeply affected by your relationship with the language you use to write.

On Writing Words: A Writer's Essential Relations with Words focuses on William Stafford's definition of a writer that is the epigraph of the book.

When I first read these words, I was intrigued by the definition and decided that I would not read any further in Stafford's book until I had pondered this definition myself. This little book is the result of my pondering.

Chapter 1
Relations with Words

Definition (noun)
An explanation of the meaning of a word, phrase, etc.
A statement that defines a word, phrase, etc.
A statement that describes what something is.
A clear or perfect example of a person or thing (Merriam-Webster).

Definition of a Writer

In his book, *Writing the Australian Crawl*, William Stafford defines a writer with these words:

> A writer is a person who enters into sustained relations with the language for experiment and experience not available in any other way (Stafford 12).

Stafford's definition of a writer is unlike any other I have ever read. Most definitions define you as a writer by *what* you write and *how* you write. His definition defines you as a writer by your relationship with language. What is particularly intriguing is how Stafford's change of focus from *you as the writer*, to *you as the writer in relationship with the words you use to write*, results in an original and perceptive description of what it means to be a writer.

In Relations with Language

The critical word in Stafford's definition of a writer is *relations*. To be a writer is to be in relationship with another. The *other* is language itself. This relationship with language is the defining characteristic of all writers.

At first glance, writing looks like a lonely occupation. The writer sits alone, sometimes staring at the computer screen or the blank paper, waiting for that magical moment when inspiration strikes. Then words come. The writer fills the screen or the paper with words, words, and more words. The writer is no longer alone. Even if the writer is on an isolated island in the middle of the ocean, a writer who writes is never alone.

When you write, you are involved in a relationship with language itself. Words are not just passive tools for you to use for your own purposes. Rather, they are active participants in any writing project. If you have never thought of words as active participants in your writing, consider this reality. If you couldn't write words, you couldn't be a writer.

What follows is an invitation to celebrate the role of writing in your life, especially if you describe yourself according to the first definition of writer. If you are someone who writes—or wants to write—books, articles, poems, stories, screenplays, essays, or anything else to publish for other people to read, writing itself is the essential medium for your efforts and words are your essential partners.

Chapter 2
Relations or Relationship?

Relationship (noun)
The way in which two or more people, groups, countries, etc., talk to, behave toward, and deal with each other
A romantic or sexual friendship between two people
The way in which two or more people or things are connected (Merriam-Webster).

Relationship

In any relationship, there are always at least two participants. The relationship can be easy. It can be difficult. It can be a love affair. It can be a constant battle. The relationship can run from hot to cold and back again. The essential aspect of every relationship is that there is always another. This is why writing is never a solitary activity.

Although relationship with language defines what it means to be a writer, the importance of this relationship is often unappreciated, ignored, or taken for granted. In any relationship, the more you pay attention to the other, the more you appreciate the other, the more you love the other, the more the relationship grows, thrives, and endures. Just as friendships, partnerships, marriages, and love affairs cannot thrive when one person takes the other for granted, writers who ignore their essential relationship with language cannot thrive as writers.

Relationships are also dynamic. They change over time, growing closer or farther apart. The healthiest, happiest relationships are the ones in which the two partners in the relationship are changing in the same direction, rather than moving apart.

If you want to write well, you will become a better writer by paying close attention to your essential partner in the relationship. The more you appreciate language itself, the better writer you will become.

Relations with the language

A writer is a person who enters into sustained *relations with the language* for experiment and experience not available in any other way.

Up to this point, I have used the word relationship. However, Stafford refers to *relations* rather than *relationship*. His word choice is worth pondering here. What's the difference between relationship and relations, especially since they both mean the same thing? Both refer to interactions with others. The difference is more of connotation rather than definition.

As a word, *relations* has two distinct connotations. *Relationship* is singular. *Relations* is plural. The plural form implies multiple interactions. Relations is also a rather formal word. Countries have diplomatic relations or trade relations with each other. The other connotation of relations refers to sexual intercourse.

In contrast, *relationship* is more informal. It is singular and tends to be broader in definition, applying to any kind of interactions with others.

Whatever differences Stafford intended by his word choice, from this point onward, I will use the word relations rather than relationship to refer to any interactions between a writer and language.

If you are going to enter into sustained relations with the language, you need to understand what "the language" means by the word *relations*. It doesn't take long to discover that the language—in this case, the language is English—is not all that transparent.

The English Language

The English language comes with a past. Actually, it comes with many pasts. English is a complicated, messy language, its enormous vocabulary filled with words from its ancestors. And what a horde of ancestors they are. The family tree is anything but pure. English traces some of its words directly back to its Latin ancestors, or indirectly through other Latinate languages, such as Old French. Other words go back to ancient Germanic, Norse, or Celtic ancestors. Some are borrowed from other languages. Some go all the way back to Proto Indo-European roots.

As a matter of linguistic history, English takes words from everywhere and then claims them as its own. If those inherited words aren't enough, English speakers and writers make up new ones. Dictionaries can't keep up with the ever-rising tide of English words.

Despite this messy past, if we are going to enter into relations with English words, we need to investigate the family tree. What hidden secrets lie within these words we have claimed as our own?

Meaning of Relations

Let's start with the word *relations*. The word came from the Latin side of the family, by way of Old French *relacion,* which it borrowed from Latin *relationem,* which came from Latin *relatus*. Along the way, it carried with it two distinct meanings. The first is the "act of telling," when you *relate* a story or give a report. The second refers to "connection," used to identify your *relatives*—the people connected to you by birth or marriage.

Already, we have two distinct meanings of relations. In one, you are a storyteller. In the other, you have a family connection to another. Both meanings are relevant to your experience as a writer who enters into relations with language. When you write, you can tell the stories of the words themselves. You can also consider how words themselves create deep family bonds. Words connect you to a large family sharing a common language.

Language shapes each of us in profound ways. It begins with your identity. Who do you think you are? Why do you think that? How you think, what you think, and what you write are deeply interconnected with your own language. Language differences become cultural differences, making it harder for you to relate to people who do not speak your language. You cannot tell their stories very well and you do not feel the same "family" bonds to a culture shaped by a different language.

Enters Into

> A writer is a person who **enters into** sustained relations with the language for experiment and experience not available in any other way.

Stafford's verb choice in his definition of a writer is particularly intriguing. A writer *enters into* relations with language. "Entering into" describes a willingness to go into new territory by choice rather than obligation. His language evokes the words of the original *Star Trek* television series first broadcast in 1966—"to boldly go where no man has gone before." These words spoken at the beginning of each episode describe an explorer's willingness to enter into unknown space:

> Space: The final frontier.
> These are the voyages of the Starship Enterprise.
> Its 5 year mission.
> To explore strange new worlds.
> To seek out new life and new civilizations.
> To boldly go where no man has gone before (Star Trek).

This Star Trek introduction can be a template for a writer who is willing to enter into relations with language. As a writer, you can choose to be a voyager into unknown territory—the vastness of human languages. You can choose to study languages. You can explore the multitude of words available for you to use. You can seek out new meanings, gain new perspectives, and change your mind because of your bold explorations.

This opening statement from the television series that began in 1966 also demonstrates how the English language itself is constantly evolving over time. English speakers and writers expand their vision of current reality by changing the words they use.

By the time that *Star Trek: The Next Generation* began in 1987, the last line was no longer "where *no man* has gone before." It became "where *no one* has gone before."

The change from "no man" to "no one" was a result of growing sensitivity to the gender bias in language. This linguistic accommodation to changed social reality reflected the growing awareness of the problematic usage of the word *man*. As with so many words, the English word "man" is not simple. It can refer to any human being or it can refer to an adult male in contrast to an adult female or a child.

(And to the dismay of the grammatical purists who complained from the beginning of Star Trek about the split infinitive of "to boldly go," the infinitive remained split.)

This is how and why words change and how connotations of words change over time. This kind of change is why English is an ever-evolving, ever-changing, ever-growing language. When you write, part of your task as a writer is to enter into relations with the words you use, to discover what they once meant and what they now mean, to see how word choices can be the source of communication problems or the solution to communication problems.

Sustained Relations

> A writer is a person who enters into **sustained** relations with the language for experiment and experience not available in any other way.

Stafford chooses to describe the relations between writer and language with a single adjective, the word *sustained*.

Sustain is another word that became part of the English language from its Latin ancestor, *sustinere*, by way of Old French *sostenir*. The basic meaning is "to hold" (*tenere*) "from below" *(sub)*. To sustain is to support. The definition in English expanded to include the sense of "to continue to support" *(Online Etymology Dictionary)*.

This basic meaning of the word "sustain" means that you engage in ongoing relations with language over time. You don't just look up the meaning of a word now and then. You make study of words an ongoing process. You seek to understand their history and original meanings as you trace their development over time and place.

What is particularly interesting about the word choice *sustained* is the original Latin meaning of "continue to support." This sense of *sustained relations with the language* means you are not just looking up words for your use. You are also providing sustenance and support for the words themselves. Why does this matter? It matters because words can be misused and their original intentions lost as they are replaced by imposter meanings.

Your willingness to enter into this kind of ongoing study of the words you use expands your relations with the words you use as a writer. Just as the Star Trek voyagers were willing "to boldly go" into unexplored territory, you can be a bold explorer of the words you use. You can discover their stories as you explore their histories. You can find out where they came from and where they went. As any bold explorer can tell you, you never know what you will discover when you enter into new territory.

Experiment and Experience

> A writer is a person who enters into sustained relations with the language *for experiment and experience* not available in any other way.

The second part of Stafford's definition of a writer gives the reason why a writer would enter into relations with the language: "for experiment and experience not available in any other way."

Both "experiment" and "experience" originated in Latin *experientia,* from *ex* ("out of") and *peritus* ("tested") and found their way into English by means of Old French *esperience.* The root meaning of experience is "knowledge gained by repeated testing."

Both experiment and experience are about testing and trying things out. In contemporary English, the difference between them is a matter of connotation. "Experiment" is intentional. You try out something to observe the result. "Experience" can also be intentional. However, experience is often unintentional. You often gain the most knowledge from unintended experiences rather than controlled experiments.

Stafford makes room in his definition for both kinds of learning. Some writing projects are deliberately experimental. Writing becomes experiment when you try out words to find the ones that allow you to write what you intend to write. Willingness to experiment is why writers will rewrite and rewrite and rewrite as they try out different words to find the ones that are best able to express what the writer wants to express.

Experience is the result of such testing. When you try on words the way you try on clothing in a store dressing room, you are not simply writing to assert what you already know or believe. You are engaged in an experimental process related to language itself. This kind of testing of language can lead to unexpected results. Whatever the outcome, more experiments with language lead to greater experience with language.

Not Available in Any Other Way

A writer is a person who enters into sustained relations with the language for experiment and experience *not available in any other way.*

This is a case of expressing the obvious. Simply put, you cannot be in relations with language as a writer if you don't write.

Chapter 3
Word by Word

Word (noun)
A speech sound or series of speech sounds that symbolizes and communicates a meaning usually without being divisible into smaller units capable of independent use (Merriam-Webster).

Words

William Stafford defines a writer as a person who enters into relations with *language*. Actually, you don't enter into relations with language. Instead, you enter into relations with *the words of a language,* one word at a time.

Words are the atoms of language, the smallest indivisible units of meaning. You can break a word into its components—its letters and its syllables—but splitting a word is like splitting an atom. Just as physicists can split atoms, you can split words, but you don't have a whole entity any longer.

When you read, you can see whole chunks of language at once because you are observing words, but observing is not the same as entering into relations with another.

Consider the oceans of Earth. No one can have relations with an ocean as a whole entity. Astronauts who have gone far enough into space to look down on a whole ocean are not entering into relations with the ocean. They observe oceans; they do not enter into relations with them. On Earth, you have to enter into the space of the ocean itself to have relations with it. Whether you swim, deep-sea dive, or let a boat carry you through the waves, you are in relations with an ocean only when you enter into its space. Then you experience the ocean only a little bit at a time, not as a whole ocean.

One Word at a Time

When you write, everything you do involves your relations with words, one word at a time, as you enter into their environment. You can write only one word at a time. It's that way because we live in a sequential universe, controlled by time. When you write—whether you write by hand or type or even speak into some kind of recording device with the intention of putting it into writing later—you write one word at a time. You speak one word at a time.

You began your relations with words when you were a baby. At one point, you spoke your first word. A baby's first word is an event to be remembered by proud parents, recorded in baby books, and these days, maybe even recorded for posterity on the ever-present cell phone with built-in camera that can record every word.

Entering into relations with words is the same as any conversational relationship with anyone. If you do all the talking, you will know nothing about the other. The more you listen carefully to the other, the more you will know the other.

Words have their own origins, histories, and stories to tell if you are willing to listen. When you as a writer enter into relations with the words of a language, and allow those words to shape your thoughts, feelings, and experiences, you will change what you think, what you feel, and what you experience.

Chapter 4
Using Words

Use (verb)
To do something with (an object, machine, person, method, etc.) in order to accomplish a task, do an activity, etc. (Merriam-Webster).

How Writers Use Words

As a writer, you have different kinds of relations with words. The first is that you *use* words.

Words as Your Medium

You use words as your *medium*. Medium originated from the Latin *medius*, which means "middle," "midst," "center," "interval." A medium is the channel of communication between you and your readers.

Face to face, you can communicate with another person in many ways. You can speak. You can gesture. You can nod. You can touch. You can convey meaning with a look. When the only form of communication with another is through writing, words themselves are your only medium.

Words as Your Tools

You also use words as your *tools*. A tool is anything you use to accomplish some task.

Whoever said that "sticks and stones may break my bones, but words can never hurt me" didn't know much about words. Words can be tools to create or weapons to destroy. Words can build up or tear down. Word can hurt and words can heal. Words can libel, slander, tease, provoke, hurt, soothe, cajole, joke, amuse, enrage, encourage, sadden, gladden, and madden. You will never run out of words you can use as tools to accomplish your purposes.

Words as Your Product

Words are also a writer's *product*. When you write a book or a story or an article with the intention to publish it for other people to read, what are you offering? You are offering words you have chosen and arranged to create some finished product.

Sharpen Your Saws

Everything you do as a writer involves your use of words. The distinctive insight of Stafford's definition of a writer is that your use of words is shaped by your relations with words. Relations are two-sided, involving you and another.

As a writer, in relations with words, you have a responsibility to take care of your words and to use them well. The familiar old story about sharpening the saw captures both aspects of your responsibility.

Stephen Covey, in *Seven Habits of Highly Successful People*, tells the story this way. You are walking in the woods when you come across someone working to saw down a tree. The woodsman looks exhausted. You ask how long he has been working. The woodsman tells you, "More than five hours." You ask: "Why don't you stopping working so hard and sharpen your saw?" The woodsman answers that he doesn't have time to sharpen his saw because he is too busy working (Covey 287).

Other versions of the same idea begin with a

question to a woodsman: "How long would it take you to cut down this tree?" The woodsman answers that he would spend most of his time sharpening the saw before he started to cut the tree.

Wherever this story about sharpening the saw originated, the insight from the story for you as a writer is that your words are your saws. Saws are useful tools only if you know how to use them and keep them sharp. The time you spend sharpening your skills with words-as-saws results in less unproductive work and more productive work

At the same time, your tools need something from you. A significant part of your relations with words involving taking care of the words you use.

How to Sharpen Your Words

It's one thing to sharpen a saw. What do you do to sharpen your words? The place to put your attention is on the words you use every day. Just as a saw is the one essential tool of someone who wants to saw down a tree, words are the essential tools of writers. Instead of trying to increase your vocabulary by learning new words neither you nor most of your readers have ever heard or used before, sharpen your skills with the ordinary words.

The ordinary words are the ones you use without thinking much about them. They are also the ordinary words your readers use without thinking much about them. Don't bother learning the big words unless the big words are essential to your topic. Then find a way to explain what the big word means with simple words that everyone understands.

Looking Up the Ordinary Words

One of my own sharpening the saw practices is to look up ordinary words. You have already seen that. In conversation or writing or reading, I sometimes hear or use an ordinary word and I am suddenly curious about this word I have used for a lifetime. What does it mean? Where did it come from? How did its meaning change over time? Those words are the ones I look up in dictionaries—especially etymology dictionaries. I copy several dictionary definitions into my ever-growing file of word definitions. I always learn something about the word and its history and how it evolved over time.

You sharpen your saw—the words of your language—by learning how to use and take good care of your words.

Chapter 5
Words as Teachers

Teach (*verb*)
To cause or help (someone) to learn about a subject by giving lessons
To give lessons about (a particular subject) to a person or group
To cause or help (a person or animal) to learn how to do something by giving lessons, showing how it is done, etc. (Merriam-Webster).

What Do Teachers Do?

Words are your medium, your tools, and your final product. They can also be something else. They can also be your teachers. How can words be teachers? The answer begins with the idea of teaching itself. What do teachers do? *Teachers educate.*

This two word sentence mixes up the English language family tree. The first word is *teacher*. This word came from the Germanic side of the family, with the sense of *show*. The second word is *educate*, which came from the Latinate side of the family.

Education

Most of us have a clear idea of what *education* means—or at least we think we do. All of us have sat passively in classrooms while a "teacher" stands in the front of the room and provides information.

Even if you never went to college, you can probably conjure up an image in your mind of a learned professor standing in the front of a lecture hall. The professor imparts information to the students who listen passively. Your role as the student is to absorb the information and convince the teacher that you learned it by giving the right answers on quizzes and exams.

Did you notice the rather pompous word *imparts?* This word—as much as any word—captures the essence of how the essential meaning of *educate* has been hijacked by a method of conveying information.

If we allow the words themselves to teach us, we can see a dramatic difference between impart and educate. Both originated in Latin, and became English words by way of Old French. The difference between them is a matter of direction.

Impart

The root meaning of *impart* is "to divide what you possess," from the Latin *partire* ("to divide"). Impart carries the sense of giving part of your possessions—in the case of the learned professor, the possession is superior knowledge—to the ones who lack it. Therefore, the "teacher" doles out knowledge to the students.

Educate

In contrast, *educate* is derived from *educere,* which means "to lead out of." You see the meaning of the root in the word *duct.* English uses the root *duct* in a wide array of words. For example, ducts in your house allow air to flow from your furnace or air conditioner to other parts of the house. Anytime you see an English word with "duct" in it, the word describes movement either away from you or toward you.

For example, the gym I use regularly has two machines for leg work with "duct" in their names.

One is an *abduction* machine. The other is an a*dduction* machine. On the abduction machine, you push your knees apart from each other (*ab* means "away from"). On the adduction machine, you push your knees toward each other (*ad* means "toward").

Leading Out Of

What do the words themselves teach you about the essential meaning of education? Educators "lead out of." You might be asking: Lead what out of what? Educators are not conveyer belts of information, with the flow of information going in the direction of teacher to student. Instead, educators are guides who draw knowledge out of their students. Perhaps the best known example of "leading out of" is the Socratic method of teaching. In this method, the teacher engages students in dialogue by asking questions intended to teach critical thinking.

The contrast between the lecture hall method and the Socratic method concerns the source of the answers. The difference between the two is a matter of direction—the contrast between traffic flow on one-way or two-way streets. When pompous professors impart information, the answers flow from professor to students. A student learns the answers as unquestioned information. In contrast, the best teachers—including the best professors—do something quite different. They "lead out of" their students by asking questions through an interactive dialogue process.

What Can Words Teach Writers?

How does any of this apply to you as a writer in your relations with the words of a language? The question at this point concerns only your relations with language. It does not concern your relations with your readers.

To consider this question, I ask you to stretch your imagination a little bit, and see words as persons—true teachers who will engage in dialogue with you. Obviously, this words-as-persons analogy shares the characteristic of all analogies. If you push it too far, it falls apart. But if you are willing to let an analogy be an analogy, you have much to gain by thinking of words themselves as your teachers.

From this perspective, your relations with words are dynamic, ongoing, and two-directional. Words have much to teach you if you are willing to learn from them. At the same time, words are not your masters.

Words are finite creations. They are as limited by time and location and culture as any human being. And yet, words can be marvelous teachers if you allow them to teach you.

We use words as tools to tell stories. Let's turn things around and tell stories about words. Remember that the first meaning of relations is the "act of telling."

The Life Stories of Words

Every word in the language has its own story, which includes its birth, its life, and its growth. Some words become obsolete and die. They might still be on the pages of dictionaries, but no one uses them anymore. Then there are the words that don't mean what they used to mean.

Pick a word. Almost any word will do. Don't pick a big fancy word with so many syllables that you have to take a deep breath to pronounce it. And don't pick a new word that someone made up a little while ago. Instead pick a simple word that has been around for a long time. Pick a word you have known for most of your life. The kind of word you would never look up in a dictionary because you already know what it means. That kind of word. Just pick one and then look it up in a dictionary. Better yet, look it up in an etymological dictionary.

Investigate the life history of the word. See where it came from, what it meant, and what it now means. When did it become a word in English? Has the meaning changed over time? How many meanings are there? Are there meanings of the word you didn't know before?

If you let them, words can educate you by changing your perspective on how you look at the world, what you see, and how you think.

When you enter into relations with the words themselves in an effort to understand their histories, you can let them tell their own stories. You can discover how original meanings get lost, important words become trivialized, and how words are hijacked, misused, and supplanted by other words.

Changing Your Relationship to Writing

When you change your relationship to words, you change your relationship to writing itself. You no longer have to write as the one who has all the answers—as if that were possible. Rather, you can write as the one who is willing to learn anything.

Two great dynamic forces in nature are expansion and contraction. Writing involves both. You use contraction to focus on one topic, one function, one purpose. At the same time, you use expansion to broaden your vision about your topic, function, or purpose by carefully studying and choosing the words you use.

Getting the Words Right

In an often quoted interview with George Plimpton of the *Paris Review*, the renowned writer Ernest

Hemingway made this comment about choosing words:

> Paris Review: How much rewriting do you do?
> Hemingway: It depends. I rewrote the ending to *A Farewell To Arms*, the last page of it, thirty-nine times before I was satisfied.
> Paris Review: Was there some technical problem there? What was it that had stumped you?
> Hemingway: GETTING THE WORDS RIGHT (Cheney, Introduction, no page number).

This phrase can be turned around. How do you get the words right? You use the right words. The only way you can use the right words is to know what the words mean.

Chapter 6
Words Separate

Separate (verb)
To cause (two or more people or things) to stop being together, joined, or connected
To make (people or things) separate (Merriam-Webster).

Communication

A great paradox lies at the heart of language. The function of writing is to make language visible, but what is the function of language itself? The ability to use language is uniquely human. Language allows us to *communicate* with each other by means beyond noises, gestures, or pictures. But what does communicate mean?

The word itself teaches us its meaning. It's an old word, with a venerable history and deep roots. It is derived from the adjective, *common*.

Common is another word with Latin roots that entered English by way of Old French. Latin itself derived the word from earlier Indo-European words.

It means "belonging to all." Communication means "to make common."

Separation

The great paradox is that language communicates by separation. Far from making speech common— shared by all—language itself separates us by the words we use. This is because the basic function of words is to separate.

We consult dictionaries to define words, thinking that humans are the ones who define their meanings, but while we are defining words, words are defining our world.

The English word *define* is derived from Latin *definire*, from *finis* ("boundary," "end") by way of Old French *defenir*. To "define" is to set a boundary, to draw a line around something.

Although Eastern thought claims that all notion of separation is illusion, the world as we experience it is composed of a multitude of distinct entities. If all that exists is truly one, you would never know it by looking around you. Everywhere you look, you see an endless array of differences. Language—any language—does its best to acknowledge and name the differences.

Naming

Something within human beings compels us to name everything we experience. What are words except human efforts to put a name on something? The *something* can be an object, a feeling, a belief, an action, a condition, an experience. If a word exists to describe something, it's because some human being somewhere attached a name to that something.

Consider what language does with the living creatures called birds. Every language spoken by people who know that birds exist has a word for bird.

But is one word enough? Can one word describe the differences between a hummingbird and a vulture? Between an eagle and an emu? Between a crow and a sparrow? The answer is no. When it comes to defining birds, the word *bird* is nowhere nearly enough. So people create words to describe each type of bird they experience. But they don't stop by using different words to define the difference between a crow and sparrow. They also have to define the differences between various species of sparrows. The making of distinct words to define differences never ends because there is never an end of things to define.

New Words

We also need new words as our creations increase. Consider these three words: *telephone; telegraph; television*. These words combine inherited words to describe new creations.

Each begins with the same element, *tele* from Greek ("far off") and combines this shared element with inherited words describing speaking, writing, and seeing.

Phone in telephone has a long and complicated family tree, including Latin *fama* ("talk," "rumor," "reputation") and Greek *phone* ("voice," "sound"). A telephone is for speaking from afar.

Graph in telegraph also has deep roots, including

the Greek *graphein* ("write, to draw," and even earlier, "scrape," or "scratch," going back to its earliest Proto Indo-European meaning of scratching characters on clay tablets. A telegraph—technology that is outdated in our electronic age—is for sending written messages from afar.

Vision in television comes from the Anglo-French *visioun,* which was derived from the Latin root *visio* ("act of seeing"). A television is for seeing from afar.

Naming Experiences

Language does more than describe the living creatures we see and the objects we create. Language also attempts to name other experiences. These experiences are intangible states of being that we feel but cannot see. We create words to describe emotions such as anger, fear, grief, sadness, joy, happiness.

Each of these words names by a process of separating one emotion from another by identifying it with a different word. They are different words because they describe different emotional experiences.

We also create words to describe the sounds we hear, the textures we touch, the sensations we feel, the odors we smell. Whatever "it" is, if we experience it, we will find a way to name it. Naming identifies the uniqueness of each object, creature, and experience. Naming sets the boundaries between one thing and another, between one living entity and another, between one object and another, between one emotion and another.

This is why you have a name. Your name defines you—it draws a line around your identity to separate you from everyone else.

Do You Know Its Name?

Wherever you are right now, stop and look around you. Look at everything you see. Is there anything that you cannot identify with a name? Even if you don't know its precise technical name, you know a name for its general category.

Each profession, each craft, each activity has a unique set of words to describe what it does. It names its tools, its purposes, its processes, and its creations.

If you go into a hardware store and walk down an aisle filled with nuts and bolts and screws and nails, you might not know the exact name of each type of fastener, but you probably know the general category. Even if you know the difference between a nail and screw, you might not know the difference between a roofing nail and a finishing nail or a lag screw and a machine screw. However, if you don't know their specific names, the people who use these fasteners do know their names.

This uniquely human need to name what we see is inherent in what makes us human. It's the essence of what allows us to communicate clearly and precisely with others. You communicate—to make your meaning common—by using your words to separate, define, and make precise what you mean. If you intend to communicate clearly, your first task as a writer is to choose the words that will best communicate your intended meaning.

Chapter 7
The Right Words

Right (*adjective*)
Morally or socially correct or acceptable
Agreeing with the facts or truth: accurate or correct
Speaking, acting, or judging in a way that agrees with the facts or truth (Merriam-Webster).

What Are the Right Words?

Your task as a writer is to communicate to your readers exactly what you intend as clearly as possible. Words are your only medium for doing that. Whether or not you can express exactly what you intend in a way that your readers grasp your meaning comes down to the words you use. This is why Hemingway was willing to rewrite the ending of *A Farewell To Arms* thirty-nine times. He wanted to get the words right. What Hemingway didn't say is that getting the words right means choosing the right words. The right words are the ones that communicate clearly and accurately what you want to write.

This is where the quality of your relations with language matter. If you allow words to teach you, you will use them carefully and correctly. Using words correctly goes beyond correct spelling and grammatical usage. Correct spelling and grammatical usage do matter, but they are not enough for clear communication.

Respect Your Words

Using words correctly also means that you use words respectfully. *Respect* is another important word to add to your writer's toolbox. English acquired the word from Latin *respectus* by way of Old French. It means "to look back." (from *re-* "back" and *specere* "look at"). In English, the word took on the sense of "refrain from injuring." Respect is esteem for the worth or power of someone or something.

Treating words with respect means that you give them the status they deserve. Put another way, you don't use elegant and powerful words trivially. Rather, you treat your words with the dignity they deserve.

Awesome

For example, consider contemporary use of the word *awesome*. The word came from the Proto-Germanic side of the family, where it meant *fear*. In English it took on the sense of *profoundly reverential.*

Awesome is an appropriate word to describe something truly fearsome, something that deserves profound reverence. I clearly remember a powerful experience of the meaning of awesome.

When our two children were four and six, my husband and I took them on a boat tour on the Niagara River. When we boarded the boat, we each got a rain slicker and hat. Black for adults. Yellow for children. They were still cold and damp from the last tour. The sturdy Maid of the Mist carried us a short distance up the river to the base of the American Niagara Falls.

We stood on the deck as the Maid of the Mist approached the waterfall. The sound of crashing water grew louder as we got closer. The spray soaked us—to call it "mist" is a gross understatement. The engine strained mightily against the current, the loud throbbing of its engine competing with the roaring of the rushing water. We got close enough to the waterfall to see only a massive wall of water in front of us.

I looked down at my four year old daughter standing beside me. Her glowing wet face surrounded by the yellow rain hat looked like a grinning jack-o'lantern. She stared up at the wall of water crashing down before us. I saw no fear on her face. Hers was the face of awe. In the presence of a waterfall that is worthy of both reverence and fear, she looked with wonder and amazement at the truly awesome sight before her.

Regrettably, something happened to the word *awesome* in recent years. The Online Etymological Dictionary has this to say about the word *awesome*.

> awesome (adj.)
> 1590s, "profoundly reverential," from awe (n.) + -some (1). Meaning "inspiring awe" is from 1670s; weakened colloquial sense of "impressive, very good" is recorded by 1961 and was in vogue from after c.1980.

When used respectfully, *awesome* is a word with a

powerful meaning. However, if you get the kinds of emails I get, you will see claims on a daily basis about the "awesome" product or the "awesome" webinar, or the "awesome" teleseminar. You will even hear people talk about "awesome" pizza. If you hear it spoken, the word is pronounced with an exaggerated emphasis on the first syllable. "It is AWEsome!!!"

The word awesome is so overused and trivialized that the essential meaning of the word is lost. If some product for sale—including pizza—is described as "awesome," what word is left to describe the experience of being on the deck of small tour boat straining against the violent torrent created by Niagara Falls as you gaze up at one of the world's truly awesome sights, knowing that you and your little boat are no match for the power of the water?

In contrast with the truly awesome qualities of Niagara Falls, no webinar, product, or pizza—no matter how good—deserves the description of "awesome." The word awesome deserves better. And you as a writer deserve better too. If you use such a word to describe mundane things, what word do you have left to describe what is truly wondrous?

Incredible and Amazing

Awesome is just one of the words that jangle every time I see them written or hear them spoken with breathless wonder in a way that demeans the words themselves. The webinar is AWESOME! The product is INCREDIBLE! The meal was AMAZING!

Every time a writer uses such a word to describe something that doesn't deserve it, the writer is demonstrating great disrespect for words. That disrespect robs the language of a word to describe what does deserve it. And to the eyes and ears of someone who truly loves the English language in all of its complexity, you have diminished your own credibility as a writer.

You especially lose some of your credibility every time you proclaim that something or someone is "INCREDIBLE!!!" *Credible* means "believable," from the Latin *credibilis,* which means "worthy to be believed." In contrast, *incredible* means "unbelievable," from Latin *incredibilis,* which means "not worthy of belief." When you proclaim that someone is "incredible," the word you use declares that the person is not worthy to be believed. It's one thing if you really mean that you think that person is lying. It's a different matter if you intend to praise someone.

How about the latest "AMAZING" product? What does *amazing* mean? The clue is in the word *maze.* You know what a maze is—a confusing structure, where it's easy for you to lose your way. As a word, *maze* comes from the Old English side of the family. It's about being confounded and confused. The prefix *a* added a sense of wonder to the idea of being confused. The result is an English word that means "overwhelmed with wonder." Do you really intend to write that someone or something has left you confused with wonder?

Protecting Your Inheritance

The question in all of this is: Are you demeaning a word by the way you use it? Does the word itself deserve better? Would you serve warmed up pizza on the Waterford crystal you inherited from your grandmother? Would you wear her antique satin wedding gown to wash your car? Would you cover over the original Van Gogh painting of a sunflower that you inherited from your grandfather with your own acrylic painting of a dandelion?

Words are inherited too. As heirs of the language and as writers in relations with language, we owe it to the words to treat them respectfully. If you use the best words on mundane things, what do you have left to describe what is truly awesome?

Chapter 8
Making Words Invisible

Invisible (*adjective*)
Impossible to see
Not visible (Merriam-Webster).

A Paradox

After all of this attention on words, it's time for another paradox about language and its words. The function of writing is to make language visible. As a writer, you make language visible by writing words. The paradox is that the craft of writing well makes your words invisible.

You might think that these two statements look like doublespeak—the use of language with more than one meaning that is used to trick or deceive people. That is not at all what I mean here.

An example will explain what I do mean. A friend loaned me a novel about a topic that she thought might interest me. I started to read it but didn't get very far. Even though I came from an academic background and have read my share of dull books swollen with big words, I don't remember ever reading a book where I was so distracted by the writing itself that I couldn't pay attention to the story.

I had the sense that the writer wrote the book with a thesaurus beside him and stopped with every other word to look up yet another impressive word. The writer's use of language was something like a flashing billboard proclaiming: "Look at my big words! See what a great writer I am! I bet you don't even know that word, do you? Aren't you impressed?" I wasn't.

The writer made the words so visible that they interfered with the story itself. All I could see was a writer trying too hard to impress with his writing techniques and his word choices. The story got lost because the writer was attempting to show off his knowledge of big words. I stopped reading and returned the book.

Simple Words

Most writing is better with simple words. One of

Hemingway's great skills as writer was to use simple words to tell stories skillfully with exactly the right words.

When you write, your foundational goal is to communicate with your readers as clearly as possible so they will understand exactly what you intend. You don't do that with the big words that distract and confuse and call attention to themselves. You do it with the ordinary words so your readers don't think about your words as words. Instead, they get caught up in the story you are telling or what you are writing about your topic. The words are tools in the service of a larger purpose.

Good writing is like good acting. When you watch the best actors, you don't pay attention to acting technique. Instead, you get involved with the story as the actors become the ones who live out the story in front of you. A well-chosen actor so inhabits a role that you can't imagine anyone else playing the role. It's only later, as you remember the story you saw played out before you, that you might think about what a great story it was, how well it was told, how the actors were perfectly chosen for their roles, and how well the actors performed.

A well-chosen word is like a well-chosen actor. When you write, the actors of your story are the words you use. If you choose them wisely, they will accomplish your purpose without calling attention to themselves.

The more you can make your words invisible, the better your writing can accomplish your purpose. Of course, you don't actually make your words invisible. Words are your medium, your tools, and your final product. They are printed on the page or they appear on a screen, but well-chosen words do not call attention to themselves as individual words. They work together to serve the purpose of your writing.

Chapter 9
Private Words and Public Words

Publish (transitive verb)
To make generally known
To make public announcement of
To disseminate to the public
To produce or release for distribution
To issue the work of (an author) (Merriam-Webster).

Your Intention

Up to this point, we have focused exclusively on you as a writer and your relations with words. All of this focus on you and your words makes it easy for writers to lose track of another type of relations—your relations with readers.

This leads us to a significant distinction. Do you intend your writing to be private or public?

Private is derived from the Latin *privates* ("set apart," "belonging to oneself"). In contrast, *public* refers to what belongs to people in general. To *publish* is to make publicly known.

By definition, private writing is for you. Your private writing can take the form of a journal you keep on a regular basis. Private writing can be what you write down when you want to clarify what you think, express what you feel, or write down what you would really like to say to someone else. Whatever form it takes, private writing is between you and your words. You don't intend it ever to be read by anyone else.

Public writing goes beyond you and your words. If you are writing for publication, you are writing something for other people to read. Your words—all of your carefully chosen words that are both your tools and your teachers—become the medium you use to communicate with other human beings. Then your relations with your readers are relations through the means of words.

I mention this distinction between private and public writing here because recognizing this distinction was an important moment in my own development as a writer. The difference might already be obvious to you. It wasn't obvious to me for a long time. Not knowing the difference was a blind spot in my early efforts to write. I thought I was writing for publication. With hindsight, I realize I was actually writing for myself. This is why none of the many, many pages I wrote ever reached the point of being publishable.

How to write for publication is beyond the focus this little book. However, it's valuable to be clear in your own mind when you intend the words you write to be for your eyes only and when you intend them to be read by other people.

Conclusion

On Writing Words: A Writer's Essential Relations with Words is an appreciative reflection on the words by William Stafford:

> A writer is a person who enters into sustained relations with the language for experiment and experience not available in any other way.

Rather than define writers by what they write, or to broaden the meaning so that anyone who writes anything with a pen or pencil or produces words on a computer screen is designated as a writer, Stafford defines writers by their "sustained relations with the language."

This definition is intriguing enough, but the word that first captured my attention was the word *relations*—why did he choose "relations with language" rather than "relationship with language?"

After I decided that I would not reader further in Stafford's book until I had pondered this definition myself, I allowed the words of the definition to guide me. The result is both profound respect for Stafford's definition and a conviction that there is an essential element missing in his definition of a writer.

"Enters into relations with language" is formal language. Its formality evokes images of diplomats holding frustrating meetings around a truce table to negotiate the end of the latest destructive war, when the primary goal becomes saving face rather than ending carnage.

The language of "experiment and experience" also sounds very clinical and practical. *Experiment* evokes images of scientists in white coats who try out different drugs on lab rats to determine which ones survive longest and which ones die first. *Experience* can be reduced to a matter of putting in enough time and work to become proficient.

It's all very practical, very formal, very precise. And yet...something is missing in all of this. These words do not capture the reason why some people become writers.

The missing word is *love*. I have no doubt that Stafford truly loved to write, but he didn't refer to love in his definition.

Maybe he didn't use it because *love* is too

imprecise a word to capture in any one definition. If you look it up, you will see a wide range of meanings. The word love is too mushy, too indefinable, too broad to be much help in a clear definition of who is a writer.

Maybe he didn't use it because many of us have learned to protect what we truly love by keeping our deepest loves hidden away from critics and cynics.

Whatever Stafford's reasons to leave this word out of his definition, the reason why some people write is because they love to write. The exact definition of the word *love* is not the issue here. The experience of love is. When you love, you know it. You can't explain why you love what you love. You just do.

For some people who write, writing is a tool to accomplish some purpose. It is practical, necessary, and often a chore. They write because they have to write.

For others, to be a writer is to have a love affair with words. These are the people who truly love to write. They love words. They love writing itself.

They become involved with language because they love it.

If you are this kind of writer, you don't need a definition to tell you what to do. If you are in a love affair with words, you already know what to do. You give the best of what you are to the ones you love and intend the best for your beloved. You give your time, your attention, your intellect, your heart, and your soul to the words you love and you write because you love to write.

References

Cheney, Theodore A. Rees. *Getting the Words Right: How to Rewrite, Edit & Revise.* Cincinnati, Ohio: Writer's Digest Books, 1990.

Covey, Stephen. *The Seven Habits of Highly Effective People: Restoring the Character Ethic.* Fireside Book. New York: Simon & Schuster, 1989.

Martin, Gary. "To boldly go where no man has gone before." The Phrase Finder. http://www.phrases.org.uk/meanings/385400 (accessed March 5, 2014).

Stafford, William. *Writing the Australian Crawl: Views on the Writer's Vocation.* Poets on Poetry. Ann Arbor: The University of Michigan Press, 1977.

Online Dictionaries

Dictionary.com http://dictionary.reference.com/ (accessed March 5, 2014).

Harper, Douglas. Online Etymology Dictionary.
http://www.etymonline.com/
(accessed March 5, 2014).

Merriam-Webster.
http://www.merriam-webster.com/
(accessed March 5, 2014).

About the Author

Dr. Kalinda Rose Stevenson is an award-winning author, whose published writings include both academic and non-academic books, ebooks, articles, newsletters, videos, webinars, and online articles and blog posts on personal development, financial awareness, writing skills, storytelling, and biblical and theological issues.

She earned her Ph.D. at the Graduate Theological Union in Berkeley, California, in cooperation with the University of California at Berkeley.

She is a former teacher of university and theological seminary students, writing coach, and book editor. Most of all, she is a writer who loves to write.

She encourages writers to develop clarity of expression and thought, creativity, courage, and authentic writing voices.

ABOUT THE AUTHOR

Find out more at:

KalindaRoseStevenson.com

BookWritingMadeSimple.com

ABKAPublishing.com

Index

A

A Farewell to Arms, 53
academic, 75
   books, 75
accomplish your purpose, 30, 64
act of telling, 15, 40
acting
   good, 63
actors, 63, 64
amazing, 58, 59
ancestors, 4, 14
appreciation
   expand your appreciation, xv
atoms of language, 25
awe, 56
awesome, 55, 56, 57, 58

B

baby, 27
birds, 47
boundary, 46

C

Celtic, 14
choosing the right words, 53
clarity, 75
clay tablet, 5, 49
common, 1, 16, 45, 46
communicate
   make your meaning common,
      51
communicates
   by separation, 46
communication, 3, 19, 29, 45, 46,
   51, 53, 63, 66
   clear, 54

connection, 15
connotation, 13, 19, 22
contraction
   focus, 42
craft of writing well, 61
create words, 47, 49, 50
creations, 48, 51
cursive writing, xiii

D

define, 7, 46, 48, 51, 69
   the differences, 48
defining, 2, 8, 46, 47
defining birds, 47
defining characteristic, 8
defining words, 46
defintion
   dictionary definitions, 33
dictionaries, 15, 33, 40, 46, 73
   etymological dictionary, 41
   etymology dictionaries, 33
differences, 13, 16, 47
dignity, 54
direction, 12, 37, 38
doublespeak, 61
duct, 37

E

Eastern thought, 46
educate, 35, 36, 37
   essential meaning, 36
education, 36
   lead out of, 37, 38, 39
emotions, 49
English, 2, 3, 14, 15, 18, 19, 21,
   22, 35, 36, 37, 41, 45, 46, 54,
   55, 58, 59
entering into

relations with words, 27
enters into, 7, 12, 16, 19, 21, 23, 25, 26, 69
essence, 2, 3, 36, 51
essential, 1, 2, 3, 9, 11, 12, 32, 33, 36, 38, 57, 69
  essential meaning of education, 38
expansion
  broaden vision, 42
expansion and contraction, 42
experience, 21, 22, 70
experiment, 7, 12, 16, 19, 21, 22, 23, 69, 70
experiment and experience, 7, 12, 16, 19, 21, 22, 23, 69, 70
experimental, 22, 23

F

focus
  change of, 7
formal language, 70
foundational goal, 63
function of words, 46
function of writing, 45, 61

G

Germanic, 14, 35, 55
grammatical, 18, 54
graph, 48
Greek, 48, 49

H

hardware store, 51
heirs of the language, 60
Hemingway, Ernest, 43, 53, 63
how you write, 7
human, 3, 4, 6, 17, 18, 40, 45, 47, 51, 66
humans, 46

I

identity, 1
  your, 16, 50
impart, 36, 37, 39
impermanent, 4
incredible, 58
indivisible units, 25
information, 4, 6, 36, 38, 39
inherited, 14, 48, 60
intend
  your writing to be private or public, 65
intentional, 22
invisible, 64
  craft of writing well makes your words invisible, 61

L

language, 7, 1, 3, 4, 6, 7, 8, 12, 13, 14, 16, 17, 18, 19, 20, 21, 23, 25, 34, 39, 45, 46, 47, 49, 58, 61, 62, 69, 70, 72
  ability to use language, 45
  boundaries of language, 5
  function of language, 45
  spoken language, 3
  written language, 5
languages, 14, 17
Latin, 2, 3, 14, 15, 19, 20, 21, 29, 36, 37, 45, 46, 48, 49, 54, 58, 65
Latinate
  your story, 14, 35
lingua, 3
linguistic history, 14
literate culture, 5
local, 4
lonely occupation, 8
love, 11, 12, 70, 71, 72

M

man, 17, 18, 73
medium, 3, 4, 5, 9, 29, 30, 35,
    53, 64, 66
motivation, 4

N

name, xii, 47, 49, 50, 51
    defines you, 50
    everything, 47
    other experiences, 49
names, xiii, 37, 49, 50, 51
naming, 47, 49, 50
    sets the boundaries, 50
Niagara Falls, 55, 57
Norse, 14

O

observing words, 25
ocean, 8, 26
Old French, 14, 15, 19, 21, 36,
    45, 46, 54

P

paradox, 45, 46, 61
participants
    active, 8
permanent, 4
phone, 48
pizza, 57, 60
Plimpton, George, 42
private, 65, 66
private writing, 66
Proto Indo-European, 14, 49
public, xi, xii, 65, 66
public writing, 66
publish, 9, 30, 65
purpose
    of your book, 64

Q

quality of relations with
    language, 54

R

read
    how to read, xii, xiv
read and write, 5, xi
relations, 8, 13, 14, 15, 16, 17,
    19, 20, 21, 23, 25, 26, 27, 29,
    31, 32, 39, 40, 41, 65, 66, 69,
    70
    sustained relations, 7, 12, 14,
        16, 19, 20, 21, 23, 69
    two-sided, 31
    your relations with your
        readers, 39, 66
relations with words, 26, 27, 29,
    31, 32, 40, 65
relationship, xiv, 1, 2, 3, 6, 7, 8,
    11, 12, 13, 42, 69
    conversational, 27
    essential aspect of, 11
    essential relationship with
        language, 12
    with language, 3, 8, 11, 69
relationship to written language,
    xv, 2
relationship with the language,
    12
relationships, 12
    dynamic, 12
respect, 54
    treating words with respect, 54
rewrite, 22, 53
right words, 43, 53, 63

S

separate, 45, 46, 50, 51
separates, 46
separation

is illusion, 46
sharpening the saw, 31, 32, 33, 34
    words are your saws, 32
should, 4
Socratic method, 38
solitary activity, 11
spelling, 54
Stafford, William, 7, 6, 7, 8, 13, 16, 19, 21, 22, 25, 31, 69, 70, 71, 73
Star Trek, 17, 18, 21
    Star Trek
        The Next Generation, 18
sticks and stones, 30
storyteller, 15
sustain, 19
sustained, 7, 12, 14, 16, 19, 20, 21, 23, 69

T

teachers, 5, xii, xiii, 35, 36, 37, 38, 39, 66
    educate, 35
tele, 48
telegraph, 48
telephone, 48
television, 17, 18, 48, 49
testing, 21, 22
tongue, 3
tools
    passive, 8

U

unintentional, 22
universal, 4, 32
use words, 29, 30, 40, 54

V

visible
    make language visible, 45, 61

vision, 49
vocabulary, xv, 14, 32

W

waterfall, 55, 56
what you write, 3, 7, 16, 66
wonder, 56, 58, 59
woodsman, 31, 32
word
    demeaning a word, 59
    has its own story, 40
    life history of the word, 41
    one word at a time, 25, 26
    speak a word, 4
    well-chosen, 64
words, 1, 3, xiv, xv, xvi, 1, 3, 4, 6, 7, 8, 9, 14, 15, 16, 17, 18, 19, 20, 22, 25, 27, 29, 30, 31, 32, 33, 34, 35, 36, 37, 38, 39, 40, 41, 42, 43, 45, 46, 47, 48, 49, 50, 51, 53, 54, 58, 60, 61, 62, 63, 64, 65, 66, 67, 69, 70, 71, 72, 73
    are defining, 46
    are inherited, 60
    as teachers, xv, 35
    big, 33, 62, 63
    can educate you, 41
    essential tools of writers, 32
    finite creations, 40
    get the words right, 43, 53
    get to know the words, xv
    getting the words right, 43
    make your words invisible, 64
    new, 33, 48
    ordinary, 33, 63
    simple words, 33, 62
    spoken words, 3, 4, 5
    stories about words, 40
    take care of your words, 31
    tell their own stories, 42
    understand their histories, 41
    using words correctly, 54
    words are tools, 63

words as teachers, 40

words of a language, 25, 27, 39

words you use every day, 32

write words, xv, 9

written and spoken, 5

write, 8, 16, 19, 26, 30, 63, 64

how to write, xii

how well you write, 6

learning to write, 5

write creations, 1

writer, 7, xv, xvi, 1, 2, 3, 7, 8, 9, 11, 12, 13, 15, 16, 17, 19, 20, 21, 22, 23, 27, 29, 30, 31, 32, 39, 42, 54, 57, 58, 61, 62, 63, 65, 66, 69, 71, 72

defines a writer, 6, 7, 8, 16, 21, 25, 31, 70

defining essence of a writer, 2

definition of a writer, 9

identity of writer, 1

task as a writer, 19, 51, 53

writers

in relations with language, 60

writing, 1, 2, 3, xiv, xv, 1, 3, 4, 5, 6, 7, 8, 9, 11, 22, 27, 29, 33, 42, 48, 61, 62, 63, 66, 69, 71, 73

benefits of writing, 6

better your writing, xv, 64

change your relationship to writing, 42

role of writing, 9

writing for publication, 66, 67

writing skills, xv, 5, 32, 33, 63

Writing the Australian Crawl, 7, 73